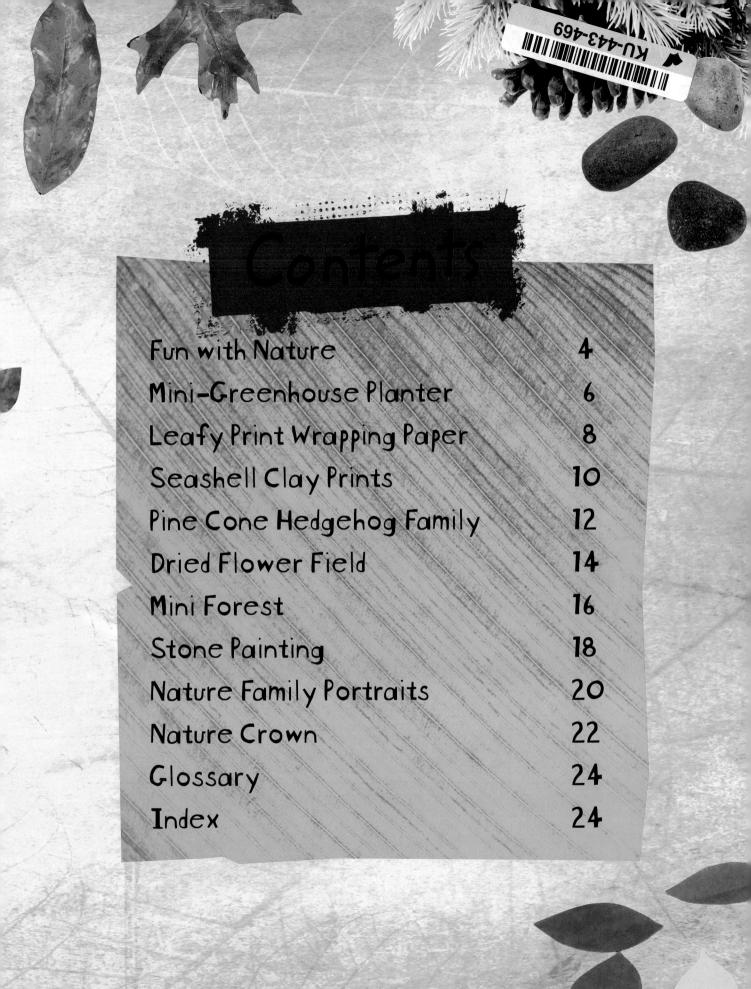

KU-443-469

Contents

Fun with Nature

You can have lots of fun with nature! You just have to step outside and look around you! Collect stones, shells, twigs and leaves when you're out and about to make fantastic pieces of art.

Be inspired by the natural world that you pass by every day. Notice the trees changing through the seasons from young, green shoots emerging in spring to the red and brown leaves falling in autumn. Every season there are new materials for you to use!

Always ask a grown up before you pick anything up. Lots of things should stay where you find them. A good rule is to only collect what has fallen from plants or trees and never pick anything that is still alive or growing. Remember to wash your findings before you use them.

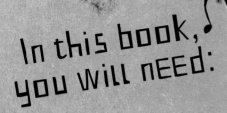

In this book, you will need:

Paint and paintbrushes
To decorate your crafts. Use poster paints or acrylic paints.

Paper or card
To display or decorate your crafts.

Clay
Air-drying clay can be found in most craft shops and even in some larger supermarkets.

Glue
PVA is a really strong glue used to stick different materials together. If you are gluing any fabric remember to use fabric glue.

Scissors
Use child-size scissors. Ask an adult to help where suggested, or on any tricky bits.

Mini-Greenhouse Planter

You will need:
One 2-litre drinks bottle
Scissors
White electrical tape or masking tape
Plastic food tray or plant pot base
Card
Sticky tape
Soil
Seeds

Nurture small seeds into little plants before you pot them outside with this indoor greenhouse! All you need is a plastic bottle, a base, some soil and some seeds!

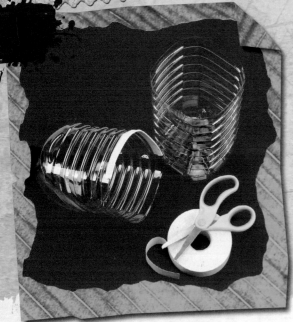

Ask an adult to cut the bottle in half. You will only need the top half for this project. Put masking tape around the cut edge to make it less sharp.

Using the tape, create the lines of your greenhouse, starting with the walls and roof.

6

There is no need to throw away the left-over plastic bottle. Try covering it in papier-mâché, leaving it to dry and then painting it to create a handy pencil pot!

Make windows and a door with the tape.

Cut some green card into the shape of grass. Stick this green card to the plastic tray.

Fill the food tray with soil and plant your seeds. Cover the seeds with the plastic greenhouse and leave to grow, watering occasionally.

Leafy Print Wrapping Paper

You will need:
Leaves
Large piece of paper
Paint
Paintbrush

Create your own unique wrapping paper all year round by using leaves you have collected from the garden or a walk in the park.

1

Choose a selection of leaves that are different shapes and sizes.

2

Paint a thin layer of paint onto one of the leaves. Remember to do this on top of a scrap piece of paper so you don't make a mess!

3

Place the painted side of your leaf onto your large piece of paper and press down lightly to create a print.

4

Repeat with different colours and leaf shapes until the whole piece of paper is covered. Leave to dry before you wrap your present!

Make your wrapping paper extra special by adding some glitter glue to the outside of the leaves to make them sparkle. Try printing onto coloured paper or even brown parcel paper!

Seashell Clay Prints

You will need:
Air-drying clay
Rolling pin
A collection of seashells
Paint
Paintbrush
Pencil
Wool or string

Make use of any seashells you find on holiday by creating a decorative clay print. Perfect to hang in your room and remind you of lovely times you had at the seaside!

1

Roll out the air-drying clay until it is about 2 cm thick.

2

Using a card template that is about 10 cm x 10 cm, cut a square shape out of the clay using an old butter knife.

3

Choose your favourite seashells and gently press them into the soft clay to make prints.

4

Use the handle of a paint brush to make two holes at the top of the tile. Leave to dry in a dry warm place for about 1–2 days.

5

Once the whole tile is completely dry, decorate using acrylic paints. Leave to dry and thread some wool through the holes to hang it up!

Pine Cone Hedgehog Family

Make your own hedgehog family using pine cones that you can find on a woodland walk!

You will need:
Pine cones
Plasticine or clay
Paint brush
Sharp pencil

1

Using some beige coloured clay, mould a cone shape for the face, two flat discs for ears and four small balls for the feet.

Pinecones are not the only natural craft material you can find in a wood; make crazy conker creatures or adorable acorn animals using the same techniques.

2

Press the cone onto the front of the pine cone until it is stuck firmly in place. Next, press the ears on top. Use the handle of a paintbrush to make a dip in each ear.

3

Use the handle of the paintbrush again to create two holes for the eyes. Carefully use a knife to create a slit for the mouth.

4

Turn the hedgehog over and press the four balls onto the bottom of the pine cone to make the feet.

5

Mould two white and two black balls for the eyes. Fill the holes you made in the cone-shaped head with the balls. Your first family member is ready! Now you can make more.

Dried Flower Field

You will need:

Flowers
Kitchen paper
Heavy books
A4 sheet of blue card
Green, yellow and white paper
Green tissue paper
Scissors
Glue

Make pretty flowers last forever by drying them out and creating a beautiful picture of a field in bloom.

Place a selection of flowers between two sheets of kitchen paper and place these between two heavy books. Leave for 2-4 weeks to dry out.

In the meantime, cut some clouds out of white paper and a wavy shape out of green paper to make rolling hills.

3

Cut out a circle from some yellow paper and some long triangles to make the sun's rays.

You could use your dried flowers for many craft projects. Make a picture of a vase of flowers or glue them onto a box to make a lovely birthday gift.

4

Cut out some stems and leaves for the flowers from the green tissue paper.

5

Glue all of the paper pieces onto the blue card. Then glue the dried flowers onto the green stems. Your picture is complete!

Mini Forest

You will need:
Twigs
String
Plastic yoghurt pot
Stones or pebbles
Green tissue paper
Glue
Scissors

Create your very own
enchanted forest inside
your house from sticks
you've collected from
your garden, park or
a walk in the woods.

Who could live in your forest? Maybe you could draw and cut out people to wander through the trees or use it as a home for the hedgehog family you can make on pages 12-13.

1

Bundle together some twigs. Tie the bundle together with some string.

2

Place the twigs in the yoghurt pot and fill it with the small stones so that the miniature tree can stand on its own.

3

Cut out small leaf shapes from the tissue paper. You can decide whether you want spring green trees, red and orange trees for autumn, or a multicoloured magical forest using blues and purple.

4

Glue the leaves onto the ends of the twigs to make full branches. Now make some more to fill your forest.

Stone Painting

You will need:
Stones, pebbles and rocks
Paint
Paintbrush
PVA glue
Googly eyes
White felt
Scissors

Create many colourful creatures by painting rocks, pebbles or stones. These buzzing bees make great ornaments, colourful bookends or pretty paper weights.

Your stone collection can be made into any animal you want. Just think about what shape stones will be best to use and what colours you'll need.

1

Choose a stone and paint it yellow. Leave to dry in a warm place.

2

Once the yellow paint is dry, paint three thick black stripes onto the stone.

3

Using PVA glue, stick two googly eyes onto the front of the stone.

4

Cut out some wings from the white felt. Glue on to the top of the stone and leave to dry completely.

Nature Family Portraits

You will need:
Leaves
Coloured and white paper
Magazines
Scissors
PVA glue
Black felt-tip pen

Create crazy family portraits by using leaves and other craft materials.

If you want your family portraits to look exactly like the members of your family, take a photograph and print them out. You can then cut out their features and stick them onto the leafy head and bodies.

20

Glue a leaf onto a coloured bit of paper. This will make the head of your portrait.

Cut out eyes, noses, mouths, ears and hair from different people in an old magazine. Choose some and glue in place on the leaf.

Once the glue is dry, cut out the head leaving a small border of coloured paper.

Glue this onto the white paper. Draw some arms and legs to create your person. Make lots of people and glue them onto the same page to make a family!

Nature Crown

You will need:
Twigs
PVA glue
Paint or glue brush
Leaves
Tissue paper
Gold card
Stapler
Plastic pocket

If you have made too many leaves or twig triangles, try gluing them onto lengths of string to make a cool hanging for your window.

Be the king or queen of the forest with this spectacular nature crown.

1

Cut the tissue paper into rectangles. Paint with glue. Lay three twigs on top in a triangle shape. Fold the tissue paper over the twigs and paint on more glue. Make about 6 triangles and leave to dry.

2

On a plastic pocket, cover a sheet of tissue paper in PVA glue. The plastic pocket makes the tissue paper easier to peel off when dry. Stick some leaves onto the sheet. Make two of these sheets in different colours.

3

Once the sheets are dry, cut the leaves out keeping a coloured border around the leaves.

4

Staple strips of gold card together to make a crown that will fit onto your head.

5

Use sticky tape or glue to attach the triangles and leaves to complete your crown.

Glossary

greenhouse a building used to grow plants all year long. They usually have a glass roof and glass walls.

nurture to encourage the growth of plants by watching and watering them when necessary

paper weight a small heavy object placed on top of papers to stop them moving in the wind or by accident

shoots a new growth on a tree or plant

template a shape used as a guide for drawing or cutting

technique a particular way of doing something

unique different from everything else

Index